THE NEW SCOTTISH SONG BOOK

Forty-five
traditional Scottish songs

Selected and arranged by
GEORGE McPHEE
GEORGE C. McVICAR
JOHN RANKIN
STUART M. ROBERTSON

Music Editors
GEORGE McPHEE
FRANK SPEDDING

The Hardie Press

Contents

Preface and Acknowledgements	1
Songs	2
Glossary	90
Index	94

The publisher acknowledges subsidy from
The Foundation for Sport and the Arts
towards the publication of this volume

© The Hardie Press, 1994

ISBN 0 946868 12 3

Originally published in 1987 by Oxford University Press

This edition published in Great Britain 1994 by
The Hardie Press, 17 Harrison Gardens, Edinburgh, EH11 1SE

Second Impression 1998

The purchase or hire of this work does not convey the right to perform it. Permission to perform the work or material from the work in public must be obtained from the Performing Right Society, 29/33 Berners Street, London W1P 4AA, or its affiliates throughout the world, unless the owner or the occupier of the premises being used holds a licence from the Society.

All rights reserved. No part of this publication may be reproduced, stored in a retrieval system, or transmitted, in any form or by any means, electronic, mechanical, photocopying, recording or otherwise, without the prior permission in writing from the publisher.

Printed in Great Britain by Martin's the Printers Ltd, Berwick upon Tweed

Preface

The present book has been compiled in the hope that it will be of use to singers, both amateur and professional, to teachers of singing, to schools, and to the hundreds who enter the competitive music festivals of Scotland and elsewhere. In other words it is a performing edition which lays little claim to scholarship. The editors are conscious, for example, that the airs for both *Auld lang syne* and *The bonnie Earl o' Moray* are not those to which the words were originally sung. Instead we have chosen the tunes with which they are now popularly associated. There is, however, a degree of authenticity in the arrangement of *Auld lang syne*, in so far as the present editor has aimed at capturing some of the sentiment Burns intended and has eschewed the casual, and sometimes inebriated, conviviality with which the song is now almost universally associated.

Of the enormous corpus of traditional Scottish songs hundreds have had to be omitted, but *The New Scottish Song Book* does not include any that are to be found in *The Saltire Scottish Song Book*. To this extent the two books complement each other and users of the present book are advised to read the preface to the previous volume for advice on lowland Scots pronunciation, alternative rhythmic patterns and suggestions about interpretation. As most of the settings are strophic there are few marks of expression; these are left to the imagination of the singer, though we have indicated some suggestions in the piano accompaniments.

In particular, the editors would like to remind singers of the wide difference in Scottish dialects and to suggest that each performer or conductor uses the dialect that sounds most natural or local to him. Most Scottish poets, Burns included, used standard English spellings, but Anglicized pronunciations tend to sound false to Scottish ears and are best avoided.

Acknowledgements

Among the many people who assisted in the initial preparation of this volume, the editors wish to express their appreciation of the contribution made by the late Robert Innes, then Director of Continuing Studies at the University of Stirling, Julian Elloway, Senior Music Editor at the Oxford University Press, Margaret Simpson and Iain M. White, invaluable copyists and typist, and to each other for much mutual help.

G.C.M.

1. A rosebud by my early walk

Words by ROBERT BURNS (1759-1796)

THE SHEPHERD'S WIFE
arr. G.McP.

Burns wrote the poem in 1787 as a compliment to Jenny Cruikshank, only child of a master at the High School, Edinburgh. Some editions have *d'* rather than *a* at*.

© The Hardie Press 1994

Printed in Great Britain

THE HARDIE PRESS, 17 HARRISON GARDENS, EDINBURGH EH11 1SE
Photocopying this copyright material is illegal

2. And ye shall walk in silk attire

Words by SUSANNA BLAMIRE (1749-1794)

THE SILLER CROWN
arr. G.C.M.

© The Hardie Press 1994

Photocopying this copyright material is ILLEGAL.

3. Auld lang syne

Words by ROBERT BURNS (1759-1796)

I FEE'D A LAD AT MICHAELMAS
arr. G.McP.

© The Hardie Press 1994

Photocopying this copyright material is ILLEGAL.

3. We twa ha'e paidelt i' the burn
   Frae mornin' sun till dine;
   But seas between us 'braid ha'e roar'd
   Sin' auld lang syne.
   For auld lang syne, my dear (etc.)

4. And here's a hand, my trusty fiere,
   And gies a hand o' thine,
   And we'll tak' a richt guid willie-waught
   For auld lang syne!
   For auld lang syne, my dear (etc).

5. And surely ye'll be your pint-stoup,
   And surely I'll be mine,
   And we'll tak' a cup o' kindness yet
   For auld lang syne!
   For auld lang syne, my dear (etc.)

Burns admitted to Johnson that three of the five verses were old and that the remaining two, those that refer to the pleasures of youth, were his. The tune given here is more modern than the one to which Burns originally set the words. His tune is on page 426 of the *Scots Musical Museum*.

guid willie-waught = draught of goodwill

4. Be gude to me

Words from *Christie's Collection of Traditional Ballads*

Origin of melody unknown
arr. G.McP.

© The Hardie Press 1994   Photocopying this copyright material is ILLEGAL.

5. Blythe ha'e I been on yon hill

Words by ROBERT BURNS (1759-1796)

THE QUAKER'S WIFE
arr. J.R.

Moderato (♩.= c.56)

1. Blythe ha'e I been on yon hill As the lambs before me, Careless ilka thocht and free As the breeze flew
2. Heavy, heavy is the task Hopeless love declaring; Trembling, I dow nocht but glow'r Sighing, dumb de-

© The Hardie Press 1994   Photocopying this copyright material is ILLEGAL.

6. Blythe was the time

Words by ROBERT TANNAHILL (1774-1810)

MORNIAN A GHIBARLAIN
arr. G.McP.

1. Blythe was the time when he fee'd wi' my faither, O! Happy were the days when we herd-ded the-gither, O! Sweet were the oors when he rowed me in his plaid-ie, O! An' vowed to be mine, my

(3.) pu'd me the craw-ber-ry, ripe frae the bog-gy fen; He pu'd me the straw-ber-ry, red frae the fog-gy glen; He pu'd me the rowan, frae the wild steep sae gid-dy, O! Sae lov-in' and kind was my

© The Hardie Press 1994

Photocopying this copyright material is ILLEGAL.

7. Glenlogie

Old Scottish Ballad

Scottish Air
arr. S.M.R.

3. When he cam' to Glenfeldy's door, sma' mirth was there,
   For bonnie Jean's mither was tearing her hair,
   'Ye're welcome, Glenlogie, ye're welcome,' said she,
   'Ye're welcome, Glenlogie, your Jeannie to see.'

4. Pale and wan was she, when Glenlogie gaed ben;
   But red rosy grew she whene'er he sat doun;
   She turned awa', wi' a smile in her e'e,
   'O dinna fear, mither, I'll maybe no dee!'

8. Come owre the stream, Charlie

Words by JAMES HOGG (1770-1835)

MACLEAN'S WELCOME
arr. J.R.

Non troppo allegro ($\quad = c.112$)

Come owre the stream, Char-lie, dear Char-lie, brave Char-lie, Come owre the stream, Char-lie, and dine wi' Mac-lean; And though you be wea-ry, we'll mak' your heart cheer-y, And wel-come oor Char-lie, and his loy-al train.

Last time to ⊕

1. We'll bring down the red deer, we'll
2. And you shall drink free-ly, the
3. If aught will in-vite you or

© The Hardie Press 1994

Photocopying this copyright material is ILLEGAL.

James Hogg 'versified' this song of Gaelic origin, 'sung by one of the sweetest singers and most accomplished and angelic beings of the human race'.

9. Gae bring tae me a pint o' wine

Words by ROBERT BURNS (1759-1796)

THE SECRET KISS
arr. J.R.

Moderato ($\quarternote = c.84$)

1. Gae bring tae me a pint o' wine, And fill it in a silver tassie; That I may drink, before I go, A service to my bonnie lassie. The boat rocks at the pier o'

2. The trumpets sound, the banners fly; The glitt'ring spears are ranked ready; The shouts o' war are heard afar, The battle closes thick and bloody; It's no' the roar o' sea or

© The Hardie Press 1994

Photocopying this copyright material is ILLEGAL.

The poem was written after seeing a young officer take leave of his sweetheart at the Port of Leith before embarking for foreign service.

10. Gala Water

Words by ROBERT BURNS (1759-1796)

GALA WATER
arr. G.C.M.

1. Braw, braw lads, On Yarrow braes ye wander through the blooming heather, But Yarrow braes, nor Ettrick shaws, Can match the lads o' Gala Water. 2. But

(3.)-tho' his daddie was nae laird, An tho' I hae nae meickle tocher, Yet rich in kindest truest love, We'll tent our flocks by Gala Water. 4. It

© The Hardie Press 1994

Photocopying this copyright material is ILLEGAL.

Haydn wrote 'This one Dr. Haydn favourite song'.

11. Hey the bonnie briest-knots!

Words anon.
from *The Scots Musical Museum* (1787-1803)

Melody adapted from a strathspey
of uncertain origin
arr. G.McP.

© The Hardie Press 1994   Photocopying this copyright material is ILLEGAL

These words, in the Buchan dialect, were sent anonymously to the *Scots Musical Museum*.

12. I lo'e nae a laddie but ane

Words by
REVD. JOHN CLUNIE (?1757-1819) (verse 1)
HECTOR McNEIL (1746-1818) (verses 2 & 3)

Origin of melody uncertain
arr. G.C.M.

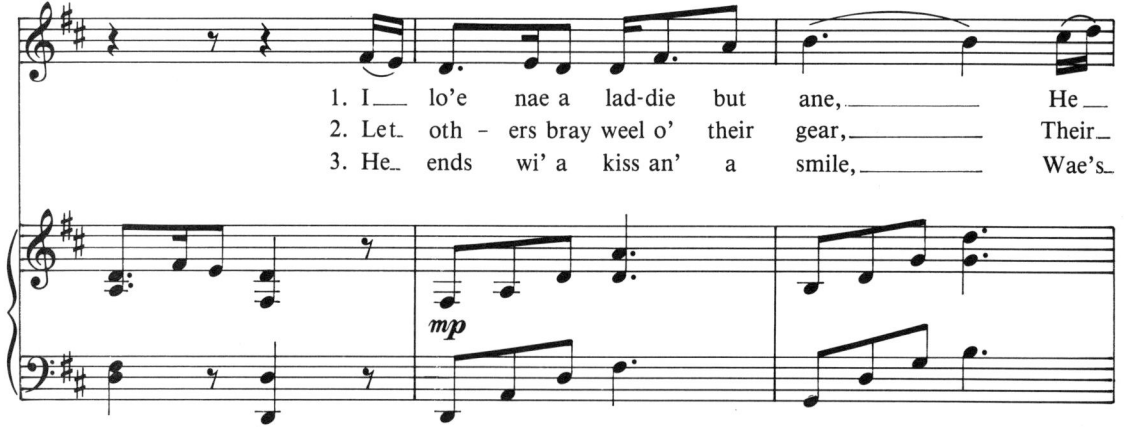

1. I lo'e nae a lad-die but ane, He lo'es nae a las-sie but me, He's will-in' tae mak' me his
2. Let oth-ers bray weel o' their gear, Their land and their lord-ly de-gree, I care nae for ought but my
3. He ends wi' a kiss an' a smile, Wae's me, can I tak' it a-miss, When a lad sae un-prac-tised in

© The Hardie Press 1994   Photocopying this copyright material is ILLEGAL.

13. I'll bid my heart be still

Words by THOMAS PRINGLE (1789-1824)

Old Border Melody
arr. G.C.M.

© The Hardie Press 1994

Photocopying this copyright material is ILLEGAL.

14. Jock o' Hazeldean

Words by SIR WALTER SCOTT (1771-1832)

Melody adapted from
THE BONY BROW
arr. G.McP.

Andante non troppo (♩ = c.46)

1. 'Why weep ye by the tide La-dye? Why weep ye by the tide? I'll wed ye to my young-est son, And ye shall be his bride; And ye shall be his bride, La-dye, Sae

2. 'Noo let this wil-fu' grief be done, And dry that cheek so pale: Young Frank is chief of Err-ing-ton, And Lord of Lang-ley dale; His step is first in peace-fu' ha', His

© The Hardie Press 1994

Photocopying this copyright material is ILLEGAL.

3. 'A chain o' gold ye shall not lack,
   Nor braid to bind your hair,
   Nor mettled hound, nor managed hawk,
   Nor palfrey fresh and fair;
   And you the fore-most o' them a',
   Shall ride our forest queen':
   But aye she lost the tears doon fa',
   For Jock o' Hazeldean.

4. The kirk was deck'd at morning tide,
   The tapers glimmer'd fair,
   The priest and bridegroom wait the bride,
   And dame and knight were there;
   They sought her baith by bower and ha',
   The Ladye was na seen!
   She's owre the border and awa'
   Wi' Jock o' Hazeldean.

15. Last May a braw wooer

Words by ROBERT BURNS (1759-1796)

THE LOTHIAN LASSIE
arr. J.R.

Giocoso ($\quarter. = c.69$)

1. Last May a braw woo-er cam' down the lang glen, And sair wi' his love he did deave me; I said there was nae-thing I ha-ted like men— The deuce gae wi' him to be-lieve me, be-lieve me; The deuce gae wi' him to be-lieve me!

2. He spak' o' the darts o' my bo-nie black e'en, And vowed for my love he was dee-in; I said he might dee when he liked for Jean— The Lord for-gie me for lee-in, for lee-in; The Lord for-gie me for lee-in!

Verses 1-7

© The Hardie Press 1994   Photocopying this copyright material is ILLEGAL.

- mor - row.

3 A well-stockèd mailen—himsel' for the laird—
  And marriage aff-hand, were his proffers:
  I never loot on that I kenned it, or cared,
  But thought I micht hae waur offers, waur offers;
  But thought I micht hae waur offers.

4 But what wad you think?—in a fortnicht or less,
  The deil tak' his taste to gae near her!
  He up the lang loan to my black cousin Bess—
  Guess ye how, the jad! I could bear her, could bear her:
  Guess ye how, the jad, I could bear her!

5 But a' the niest week as I fretted wi' care,
  I gaed to the tryste o' Dalgarnock,
  And wha but my fine fickle lover was there?
  I glower'd as I'd seen a warlock, a warlock;
  I glower'd as I'd seen a warlock!

6 But owre my left shouther I gae him a blink,
  Lest neibors might say I was saucy;
  My wooer he capered as he'd been in drink,
  And vowed I was his dear lassie, dear lassie;
  And vowed I was his dear lassie.

7 I speered for my cousin fu' couthy and sweet,
  Gin she had recovered her hearin',
  And how my auld shoon fitted her shachl't feet—
  But, Heavens! how he fell a swearin', a swearin';
  But, Heavens! how he fell a swearin'!

8 He beggèd, for gudesake, I wad be his wife,
  Or else I wad kill him wi' sorrow:
  So e'en to preserve the poor body in life,
  I think I maun wed him to-morrow, to-morrow;
  I think I maun wed him to-morrow.

Burns wrote the poem in 1787 for the *Scots Musical Museum*, but Johnson found some of it indelicate. Later he relented and published it in *Museum Vol. VI*. 'Auld shoon' is a derogatory expression for a discarded lover.

16. The Rowan Tree

Words by LADY NAIRNE (1766-1845)

Origin of melody unknown
arr. G.McP.

1. O! Rowan Tree, O! Rowan Tree, thou'lt aye be dear to me,— Entwin'd thou art wi' mony ties, o' hame and infancy. Thy leaves were aye the first o' spring, thy
2. How fair wert thou in simmer time, wi' a' thy clusters white,— How rich and gay thy autumn dress, wi' berries red and bright. On thy fair stem were mony names, which

© The Hardie Press 1994

Photocopying this copyright material is ILLEGAL.

flow'rs the sim-mer's pride;___ There_ was nae sic a bon-ny tree in
now nae mair I see,___ But__ they're en-gra-ven on my heart, for-

dim. *p*

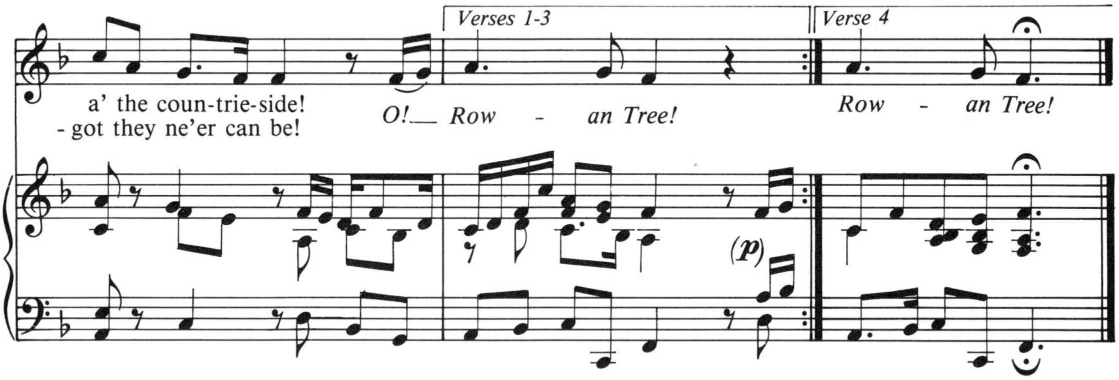

a' the coun-trie-side! O!_ Row - an Tree! Row - an Tree!
- got they ne'er can be!

Verses 1-3 | Verse 4

(p)

3. We sat aneath thy spreading shade, the bairnies round thee ran,
   They pu'd thy bonny berries red, and necklaces they strang.
   My mother! O! I see her still, she smil'd our sports to see,
   Wi' little Jeanie on her lap, and Jamie at her knee!
   O! Rowan Tree!

4. O! there arose my father's prayer, in holy evening's calm,
   How sweet was then my mother's voice, in the Martyr's psalm;
   Now a' are gane! we meet nae mair aneath the Rowan Tree!
   But hallowed thoughts around thee twine o' hame and infancy.
   O! Rowan Tree!

17. I'm owre young to marry yet

Words by ROBERT BURNS (1759-1796)

Old song or dancing tune
arr. G.C.M.

I'm owre_young, I'm owre_young, I'm

© The Hardie Press 1994   Photocopying this copyright material is ILLEGAL.

18. Leezie Lindsay

Words by
ROBERT BURNS (1759-1796) (verse 1)
ROBERT ALLAN (verses 2-4)

Highland air
arr. S.M.R.

1. 'Will ye gang to the Hielands, Leezie Lindsay? Will ye gang to the Hielands wi' me? Will ye gang to the Hielands, Leezie Lindsay, My bride and my darling to be?'

2. 'To gang to the Hielands wi' you, Sir, I dinna ken how that may be, For I ken na the road I am going, Nor ken I the lad I'm gaun wi'!'

3. 'O Leezie, lass, ye maun ken little
   If sae be ye dinna ken me;
   For I am Lord Ronald MacDonald,
   A chieftain o' high degree.'

4. She has gotten a gown o' green satin,
   She has kilted it up to the knee,
   And she's aff wi' Lord Ronald MacDonald,
   His bride and his darling to be.

A different tune and a different set of verses by Robert Gilfillan also exist.

© The Hardie Press 1994   Photocopying this copyright material is ILLEGAL.

19. O Bothwell bank

Words by JOHN PINKERTON (1758-1825)
(slightly altered)

Air by John Fergus
arr. S.M.R.

1. O Bothwell bank, thou bloomest fair, But ah! thou makest my heart fu' sair; For all beneath thy woods so green My love and I would sit at e'en. With daisies and primroses

2. He left me sad one weary day, To distant lands he sailed away, Without one word my heart to cheer, Without one kiss, without one tear. Those memories I cherish

© The Hardie Press 1994

Photocopying this copyright material is ILLEGAL.

Lyrics under the music:

twined ___ He made a gar - land my hair to bind; ___ O Bothwell
yet, ___ I would not if I could for - get. ___

bank, thou bloomest fair, But ah! thou mak - est my heart fu'

sair.   sair.

In 1783 Pinkerton published this song in his *Select Scottish Ballads*. However, the air was by John Fergus, organist of an Episcopal chapel in Glasgow. Pinkerton had to admit the forgery, but Burns deemed some of Pinkerton's ancient ballads as 'beautiful enough', forgeries or not.

20. Logie o' Buchan

Words by GEORGE HALKET (?-1756)

THE CORPORATION OF TAILORS
arr. S.M.R.

Allegretto ($\dot{} = c.112$)

1. O, Logie o' Buchan, O Logie the laird, They ha'e ta'en awa' Jamie, that delved in the yaird; Wha play'd on the
2. Tho' Sandie has owsen, has gear, and has kye, A hoose, an' a haddin, an' siller forbye; Yet I'd tak' my ain

pipe, an' the vi-ol sae sma: They ha'e ta'en a-wa' Jamie, the
lad, wi' his staff in his hand, Be-fore I'd hae him, wi' his

floo'r o' them a'. He said 'Think na lang, las-sie, tho' I gang a-
hoos-es an' land. But simmer is com-in', cauld win-ter's a-

-wa' For I'll come an' see thee in spite o' them a'.'
-wa' An' he'll come an' see me in spite o' them a'.

3. I sit on my creepie, an' spin at my wheel,
   An' think on the laddie that lo'es me sae weel;
   He had but ae saxpence he brak' it in twa,
   An' he ga'e me the half o't, when he gaed awa'.
   He said 'Think na lang, lassie, tho' I gang awa'
   For I'll come an' see thee in spite o' them a'.'

4. My daddy looks sulky my minnie looks sour,
   They gloom upon Jamie because he is puir;
   Tho' I lo'e them as weel as a dochter should do,
   They are no half sae dear to me, Jamie, as you.
   But the simmer is comin', cauld winter's awa'
   Then haste ye back, Jamie, an' bide na awa'.

Think na lang = be not weary

21. Muirland Willie

Old Scottish Ballad

THE NORTHERN LASS
arr. S.M.R.

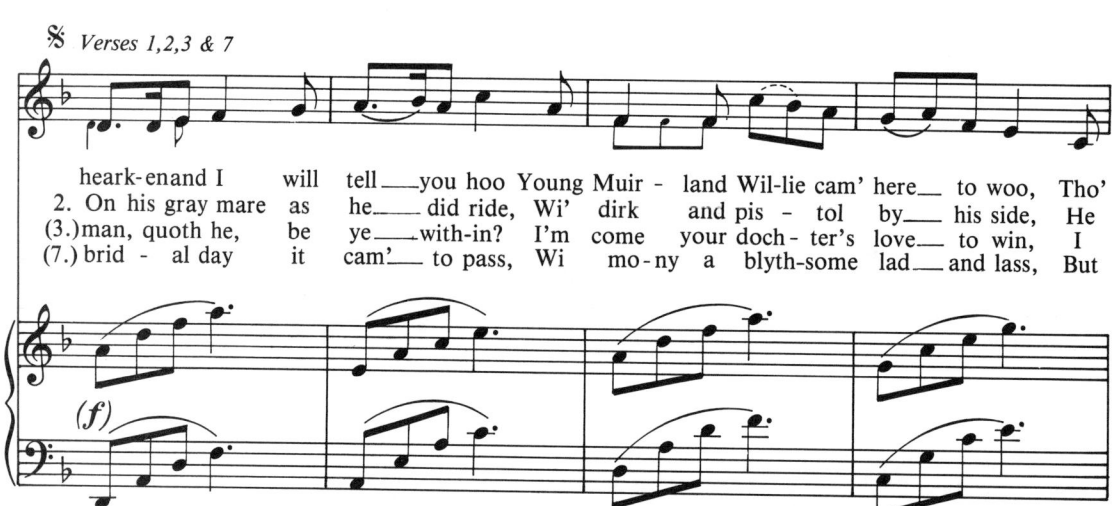

Animato (♩. = c.84)

% Verses 1, 2, 3 & 7

heark-en and I will tell you hoo Young Muir-land Wil-lie cam' here to woo, Tho'
2. On his gray mare as he did ride, Wi' dirk and pis-tol by his side, He
(3.) man, quoth he, be ye with-in? I'm come your doch-ter's love to win, I
(7.) brid-al day it cam' to pass, Wi' mo-ny a blyth-some lad and lass, But

© The Hardie Press 1994

Photocopying this copyright material is ILLEGAL.

he could nei - ther say_ nor do; The truth_ I tell_ to you._ But
prick'd her on wi' mei - kle pride, Wi' mei - kle mirth_ and glee._ Oot
care-na for mak - in' mei - kle din; What an - swer gi'e_ ye me?_ Noo
sic-can a day there ne - ver was, Sic mirth_ was ne - ver seen._ This

aye he cries, What- e'er be-tide, Mag - gie I'll ha'e to be my bride,
owre yon moss, oot owre yon muir, Till he cam' to her dad - die's door, With a
wooer, quoth he, would ye licht doun, I'll gi'e ye my doch - ter's love to win,
win - some coup - le strak - ed hands, Mess John_ ty'd up the marr-iage bands,

Verse 7 to ⊕

fal da ra, fal lal da ra la, fal lal da ra, lal da ra

Verses 2 & 3 D.S.
Verse 4 straight on

la._

(2. 𝄾)
3. Guid
4. Noo

Verses 4, 5 & 6

(4.) wooer, sin' ye are lichted doun, Where do ye win, or in what toun? I think my dochter winna gloom On sic a lad as ye. The wooer he stepp'd up the hoose, And
(5.) maid put on her kirtle broun, She was the brawest in a' the toun; I wat on him she didna gloom, But blinkit bonnilie. The lover he stended up in haste, And
(6.) maiden blush'd and bing'd fu law, She hadna will to say him na, But to her daddie she left it a', As they twa could agree. The lover he gi'ed her the tither kiss, Syne

wow— but he was wond-'rous croose,
gript— her hard a-boot the waist, With a fal da ra, fal lal da ra la, fal
ran to her dad-die, and tell'd him this,

Verses 5 & 6 repeat
Verse 7 **D. S.**

lal da ra, lal da ra la.

5. The
6. The
7. The

Last time

la.

8va

dim.

The air seems to have been known in both England and Scotland. In Ramsay's *Tea-Table Miscellany* (1724) it is described as having been known 'time out of mind'. It had also appeared in *Orpheus Caledonius* (1725) and, the tune only, as early as 1709.

22. The bonnie Earl o' Moray

Melody and words from
Hird's collection of Scottish songs Vol.I (1776)

arr. G.C.M.

Sostenuto ($\quarternote = c.54$)

1. Ye hie-lan's an' ye low-lan's, O where ha'e ye been? They ha'e slain the Earl o' Moray, An' laid him on the green. He was a braw gal-lant, An' he
2. Noo wae be to ye, Hunt-ly, An' where-fore did ye sae? I bade ye bring him wi' you, But for-bade ye him to slay. He was a braw gal-lant, An' he

© The Hardie Press 1994   Photocopying this copyright material is ILLEGAL.

rade___ at the ring; An' the bon-nie Earl o' Mo-ray, He
play'd___ at the glove; An' the bon-nie Earl o' Mo-ray, He

might ha'e been a king.
was the queen's true love. O lang will___ his la-dye Look

frae the Cas-tle Doune, Ere she see the Earl o' Mo-ray Come

cresc.

1
sound-in thro' the toon.

2 *rall.*
sound-in thro' the toon.___

'The green' is probably used for the sods of grass laid on top of a grave. 'Rade at the ring' refers to an equestrian game popular in the sixteenth century.

23. My heart's in the Highlands

Words by ROBERT BURNS (1759-1796)

CRODH CHAILEIN
arr. S.M.R.

Cantabile ($\quarter = c.72$)

1. My heart's in the Highlands, my heart is not here; My heart's in the Highlands, a-chasing the deer. A-chasing the wild deer, and following the roe, My heart's in the Highlands wher-ever I go.

2. Farewell to the Highlands, farewell to the north, The birth-place of valour, the country of worth; Wherever I wander, wherever I rove, The hills of the Highlands for ever I love.

3. Farewell to the mountains high cover'd with snow, Farewell to the straths and green valleys below; Farewell to the forests and wild-hanging woods; Farewell to the torrents and loud-pouring floods.

© The Hardie Press 1994

Photocopying this copyright material is ILLEGAL.

24. Oh, Nancy's hair is yellow like gowd

Words anon.

Old Border Melody
arr. G.C.M.

Andante e teneramente ($\quarternote = c.76$)

1. Oh, Nan-cy's hair is yellow like gowd, An' her e'en like the lift are blue, Her face is the image o' heav'nly love, An' her heart is leal an' true.

2. The in-no-cent smile that plays on her cheek, Is like the dawning morn, An' the red red blush that across it flees, Is sic as the rose ne'er has worn.

© The Hardie Press 1994

Photocopying this copyright material is ILLEGAL.

25. My only jo and dearie, o

Words by RICHARD GALL (1766-1801)

MY ONLY JO AND DEARIE, O
arr. S.M.R.

1. Thy cheek is o' the rose's hue, My only jo and dearie, o; Thy neck is like the siller dew Upon the banks sae brierie, o; Thy
2. The birdie sings upon the thorn, Its sang o' joy fu' cheerie, o; Rejoicing in the simmer morn, Nae care to mak' it eerie, o; But

© The Hardie Press 1994

Photocopying this copyright material is ILLEGAL.

teeth are o' the i-vor-y; O sweet's the twin-kle o' thine e'e; Nae joy, nae plea-sure blinks on me, My on-ly jo and dear-ie, o.
lit-tle kens the sang-ster sweet, Aught o' the care I ha'e to meet, That gars my rest-less bo-som beat, My on-ly jo and dear-ie, o.

3. When we were bairnies on yon brae,
   And youth was blinkin' bonnie, o;
   Aft we would daff the lee-lang day,
   Our joys fu' sweet and mony, o;
   Aft I would chase thee o'er the lea,
   And round about the thorny tree,
   Or pu' the wild flow'rs a' for thee,
   My only jo and dearie, o.

4. I ha'e a wish I canna tine,
   'Mang a' the cares that grieve me, o;
   I wish that thou wert ever mine,
   And never mair to leave me, o;
   Then I would dawt thee night and day,
   Nae ither wardly care wad ha'e,
   Till life's warm stream forgat to play,
   My only jo and dearie, o.

26. O Willie brew'd a peck o' maut

Words by ROBERT BURNS (1759-1796)

WILLIE BREW'D A PECK O' MAUT
Melody by Allan Masterton
arr. G.McP.

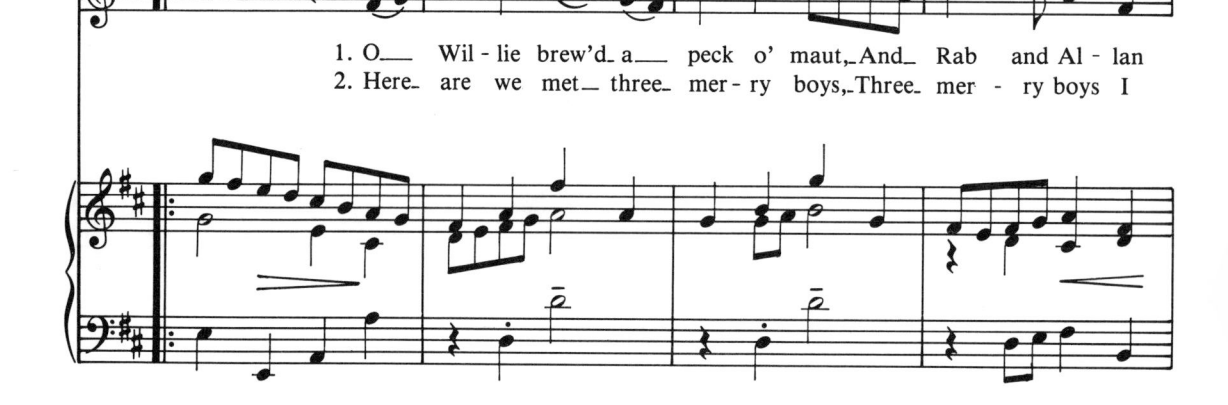

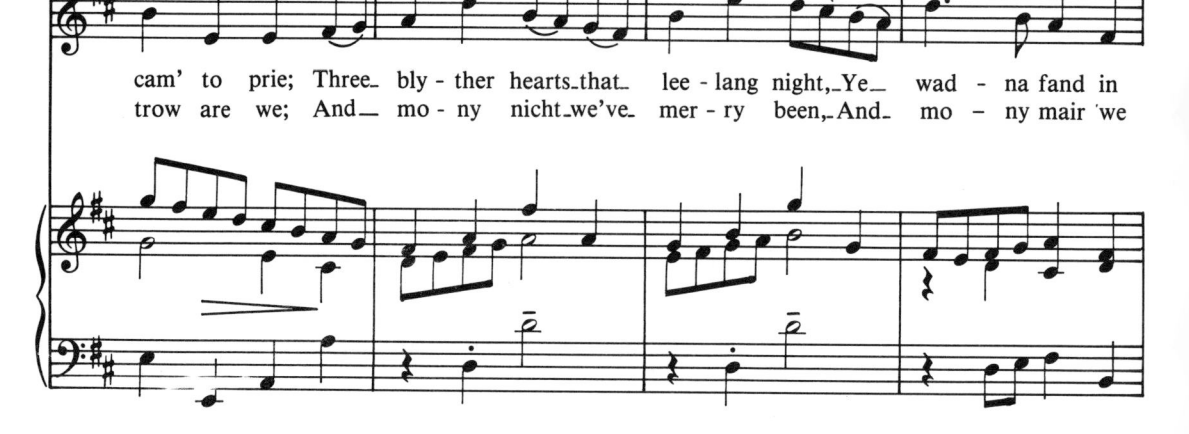

Allegro moderato ($\textit{d}$ = c.72)

1. O— Wil-lie brew'd a— peck o' maut,—And— Rab and Al-lan cam' to prie; Three— bly-ther hearts_that— lee-lang night,—Ye— wad-na fand in

2. Here— are we met— three— mer-ry boys,—Three— mer-ry boys I trow are we; And— mo-ny nicht_we've— mer-ry been,—And— mo-ny mair we

© The Hardie Press 1994   Photocopying this copyright material is ILLEGAL.

Christ-en-die. / hope to be. We are nae fou', we're no that fou', But just a wee drap in our e'e; The cock may craw, the day may daw', But aye we'll taste the barley bree.

3. It is the moon—I ken her horn,
   That's blinkin' in the lift sae hie;
   She shines sae bricht to wile us hame,
   But by my sooth she'll wait a wee.
       We are nae fou', (etc.)

4. Wha first shall rise to gang awa',
   A cuckold, coward loon is he;
   Wha last beside his chair shall fa',
   He is the king amang us three.
       We are nae fou', (etc.)

Burns wrote the words and Allan Masterton the music to 'warm his [William Nicol's] new house' in Nithsdale. The three agreed that they should 'celebrate the business'. Presumably Mr Nicol brewed the peck o' maut!

27. On Ettrick's banks

Words anon.
from *Orpheus Caledonius* (1725 & 1733)

Origin of melody unknown
arr. J.R.

1. On Ettrick's banks ae simmer nicht, At gloamin' when the sheep gaed hame, I met my lassie braw and ticht, While wand'ring through the...

2. Said I, My lassie, will ye gae To the Highland hills and be my bride? I'll bigg thy bower beneath the brae, By sweet Loch Garry's...

© The Hardie Press 1994

Photocopying this copyright material is ILLEGAL.

mist her lane. My heart grew licht, I wanted lang To
silver tide. And aft as o'er the moorlands wide, Kind

tell my lassie a' my mind, And never till this
gloamin' comes our faulds to steek, I'll hasten down the

D.C.
(Last time al fine)

happy hour, A cannie meeting could I find.
green hillside, Where curls our cosy cottage reek.

3. All day when we ha'e wrought eneuch,
   When winter frosts and snaws begin,
   Sune as the sun gaes west the loch,
   At nicht when ye sit down to spin,
   I'll screw my pipes, and play a spring,
   And thus the weary nicht we'll end,
   Till the tender kid and lamb-time bring
   Our pleasant simmer back again.

4. Syne when the trees are in their bloom,
   And gowans glent o'er ilka field,
   I'll meet my lass amang the broom,
   And lead her to my simmer shield;
   There, far frae a' their scornfu' din,
   That make the kindly hearts their sport,
   We'll laugh, and kiss, and dance and sing,
   And gar the langest day seem short.

28. Scots wha hae

Words by ROBERT BURNS (1759-1796)

HEY, TUTTIE TAITIE
arr. G.McP.

Maestoso ($\quarternote = c.66$)

1. Scots wha hae wi' Wallace bled, Scots, wham Bruce has aften led,— Welcome to your gory bed, Or to victory! Now's the day and now's the hour: See the front o' battle lour. See approach proud Edward's pow'r; Chains and slaverie!

2. Wha will be a traitor knave? Wha can fill a coward's grave? Wha sae base as be a slave? Let him turn an' flee! Wha, for Scotland's King and law, Freedom's sword will strongly draw, Freeman stand, or freeman fa', Let him follow me!

3. By oppression's woes and pains, By our sons in servile chains, We will drain our dearest veins, But they shall be free. Lay the proud usurpers low! Tyrants fall in ev'ry foe! Liberty's in ev'ry blow! Let us do or dee!

Verses 1 & 2 | *Verse 3* non rit.

© The Hardie Press 1994

Photocopying this copyright material is ILLEGAL.

29. Thou hast left me ever, Jamie

Words by ROBERT BURNS (1759-1796)

FIE HIM, FATHER
arr. G.C.M.

Doloroso (♩ = c.54)

1. Thou hast left me ev-er, Ja-mie, Thou hast left me ev-er;— Thou hast left me ev-er, Ja-mie, Thou hast left me ev-er;— Of-ten hast thou vowed that death On-ly us should se-ver;— Thou hast left thy lass for ay, I maun see thee ne-ver, Ja-mie, I will see thee ne-ver.—

2. Thou hast me for-sa-ken, Ja-mie, Thou hast me for-sa-ken;— Thou hast me for-sa-ken, Ja-mie, Thou hast me for-sa-ken;— Thou canst love an-oth-er maid While my heart is break-ing;— Soon my wear-ie eyes I close Ne-ver more to wa-ken, Ja-mie, Ne-ver more to wa-ken.—

The air *Fie him, Father* is also sung to the poem *Saw ye Johnnie cumming' quo' she,* and was lively and humorous. However, Burns saw the pathos inherent in the tune and wrote for it the two verses given here. Burns was inspired by the playing of an Edinburgh oboist, a Mr Fraser, who made the tune 'the language of despair' when he played it.

© The Hardie Press 1994   Photocopying this copyright material is ILLEGAL.

30. The banks of the Devon

Words by ROBERT BURNS (1759-1796)

THE MAIDS OF ARROCHER
arr. S.M.R.

Andante (♪ = c.92)

1. How pleasant the banks of the clear winding Devon, With green spreading bushes, and flow'rs blooming fair; But the bonniest flow'r on the banks of the Devon Was once a sweet bud on the
2. O spare the dear blossom, ye orient breezes, With chill hoary wing, as ye usher the dawn; And far be thou distant, thou reptile that seizes The verdure and pride of the

© The Hardie Press 1994

Photocopying this copyright material is ILLEGAL.

braes of the Ayr. Mild be the sun on this sweet blush'ing flow'r, In the
gar - den and lawn! Let Bour-bon ex - ult in his gay gilded li - lies, And

gay ro - sy morn, as it bathes in the dew; And gen - tle the fall of the
Eng-land, tri - umph-ant, dis - play her proud rose: A fair - er than ei - ther ad -

poco rall.

soft ver - nal show - er, That steals on the ev-'ning each leaf to re - new.
- orns the green val - leys, Where De-von, sweet De-von, me - an - dering flows.

31. The carls o' Dysart

Words by ROBERT BURNS (1759-1796)

Origin of melody unknown
arr. G.McP.

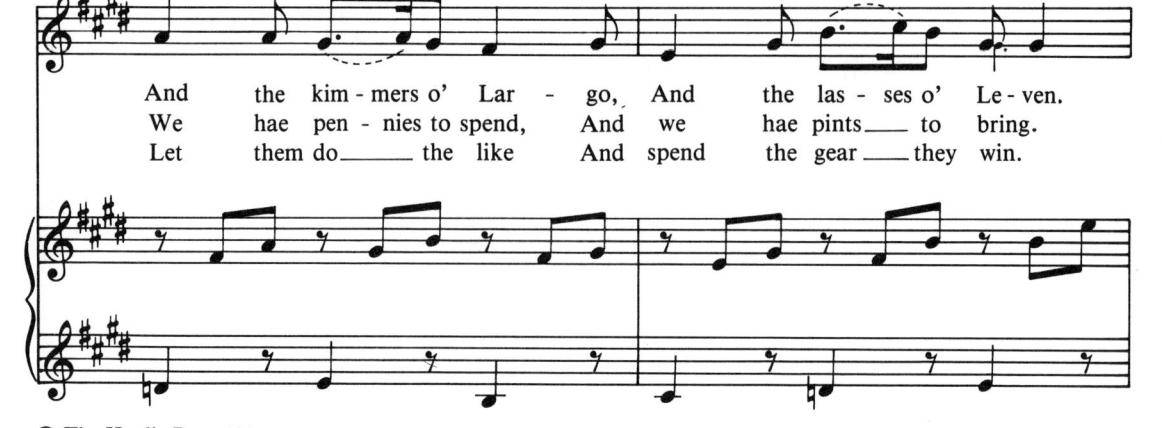

1. Up wi' the carls o' Dysart, And the lads o' Buckhaven, And the kimmers o' Largo, And the lasses o' Leven.
2. We hae tales to tell, And we hae sangs to sing; We hae pennies to spend, And we hae pints to bring.
3. We'll live a' our days, And them that come behin' Let them do the like And spend the gear they win.

© The Hardie Press 1994

Photocopying this copyright material is ILLEGAL.

Hey, ca' thro', ca' thro', For we hae mei-kle a-do;

Hey, ca' thro', ca' thro', For we hae mei-kle a-do!

Verses 1 & 2 | Verse 3

Ca' thro' = work away

32. The gallant weaver

Words by ROBERT BURNS (1759-1796)

THE WEAVER'S MARCH
arr. G.C.M.

Allegretto (♩ = c.100)

1. Where Cart rins row in tae the sea, By mony a flow'r and shading tree, There lives a lad, the lad for me, He is a gallant
2. My daddie sign'd my tocher band, To gi'e the lad that has the land, But tae my heart I'll add my hand, And gi'e it to the

© The Hardie Press 1994   Photocopying this copyright material is ILLEGAL.

weav - er. Oh I had woo - ers ought or nine, They
weav - er. While birds re - joice in leav - y bow'rs, While

gi'ed me rings and rib - bons fine, But I was fear'd my
bees de - light in open - ing flow'rs, While corn grows green in

heart wad tine, And I gie'd it tae the
sim - mer show'rs, I'll lo'e my gal - lant

Verse 1
weav - er.

Verse 2
weav - er.

33. The gloomy night is gath'ring fast

Words by ROBERT BURNS (1759-1796)

DRUMION DUBH
arr. J.R.

Con moto (♩ = c.100)

1. The gloomy night is gath'ring fast, Loud roars the wild inconstant blast, Yon murky cloud is
2. The hunter now has left the moor, The scatter'd coveys meet secure, While here I wander,

© The Hardie Press 1994

Photocopying this copyright material is ILLEGAL.

foul___ with__ rain, I see____ it__ dri - ving__
press'd with care, A - long____ the__ lone - ly__

o'er____ the___ plain.
banks____ of___ Ayr.

After last verse

3. The autumn mourns her ripening corn
   By early winter's ravage torn;
   Across her placid azure sky
   She sees the scowling tempest fly;

4. Chill rins my blood to hear it rave—
   I think upon the stormy wave,
   Where many a danger I must dare,
   Far from the bonnie banks of Ayr.

5. 'Tis not the surging billows' roar,
   'Tis not that fatal, deadly shore;
   Though death in every shape appear,
   The wretched have no more to fear:

6. But round my heart the ties are bound,
   That heart transpierced with many a wound;
   These bleed afresh, those ties I tear,
   To leave the bonnie banks of Ayr.

7. Farewell, old Coila's hills and dales,
   Her heathy moors and winding vales;
   The scene where wretched fancy roves,
   Pursuing past, unhappy loves!

8. Farewell, my friends, farewell my foes,
   My peace with these, my love with those;
   The bursting tears my heart declare;
   Farewell, the bonnie banks of Ayr.

In 1786 Burns wrote, 'I composed this song as I conveyed my chest so far on the road to Greenock, where I was to embark in a few days for Jamaica. I meant it as my farewell dirge to my native land.'

34. The lass of Patie's mill

Words by ALLAN RAMSAY (1686—1758)

Origin of melody unknown
arr. J.R.

Andante ($\quarter = c.76$)

mf

1. The lass of Patie's mill, So bonnie, blythe, and gay, In spite of all my skill, She stole my heart a-
2. Without the help of art, Like flow'rs which grace the wild, She did her sweets impart, Whene'er she spoke or
3. O! had I all that wealth, Hopetoun's high mountains fill, In-sured long life and health, And pleasure at my

© The Hardie Press 1994

Photocopying this copyright material is ILLEGAL.

way.___	When ted-dling of__ the__ hay,___	Bare-
smiled.___	Her looks__ they__ were so__ mild,___	Free
will;___	I'd pro-mise__ and__ ful-fil___	That

-head-ed__ on__ the__ green,___ Love__ midst__ her__ locks__ did__
from__ af-fect-ed__ pride,___ She__ me__ to__ love__ be-
none__ but__ bon-nie__ she,___ The__ lass__ of__ Pa-tie's__

After last verse

play,__ And wan-ton'd in her e'en.
-guiled;__ I wish'd her__ for my bride.
mill,__ Should share the_same with me.

The air is believed to date from the middle of the sixteenth century.

35. The tocherless lass

Words by MALCOLM MACFARLANE

Highland Air
arr. G.McP.

Lento ($\quarternote = c.66$)

Sheep and cat-tle I ha'e nane, O, No a cloot to ca' mine ain, O, Yet the lads are un-co fain, O, To come here a-court-in' me.

Last time to ⊕

© The Hardie Press 1994

Photocopying this copyright material is ILLEGAL.

1. But there's ain across the ocean, And o' him I
2. What tho' I've nae land to till, O, Herds or flocks up-
3. There's a charm and there's a grace, O, In my to-cher:

hae a notion; Steadfast still is my devotion
-on the hill, O, I've a tocher better still, O,
that's my face, O, And there's few aboot the place, O,

Last time

Tho' he didna marry me. - courtin' me.
That ye dinna often see.
Can at spinnin' equal me.

36. The Laird o' Cockpen

Words by LADY NAIRNE (1766-1845)

WHEN SHE CAME BEN, SHE BOBBED
arr. G.McP.

Allegretto ($\dotted{\quarter} = c.80$)

1. The Laird o' Cock-pen, he's proud and he's great, His mind is ta'en up wi' the things o' the state, He wanted a wife his braw hoose to keep, But favour wi' wooin' was fash-ous to seek.

2. Doun by the dyke side a lady did dwell, At his table heid he thocht she'd look well; Mac-leish's ae dochter, o' Cla-vers-ha' Lee, A penniless lass wi' a lang pedigree.

3. His wig was well pouther'd, as guid as when new; His

waist-coat was white, his coat it was blue; He put on a ring, a sword an' cock'd hat, An' wha could refuse the Laird wi' a' that? 4. He took the gray mare, he rade canilie, An' rapp'd at the yett o' Claversha' Lee; 'Gae tell Mistress Jean to come speedily ben, She's wanted to speak wi' the

Laird o' Cock-pen.' 5. Mistress Jean she was mak-in' the el-der-floo'r wine; 'An' what brings the Laird at sic a like time?' She aff wi' her ap-ron, an' on her silk goun, Her mutch wi' red rib-bons, an' gaed a-wa' doun. 6. An' when she cam' ben he bow-èd fu' low, An' what was his er-rand he soon let her know; A-

-maz'd was the Laird when the la-dy said 'Na!' An' wi' a laigh curt-sie she turn-èd a-wa'! 7. Dum-found-er'd* was he, but nae sigh did he gie, He mount-ed his mare an' he rade can-ni-lie; An' af-ten he thocht, as he gaed through the glen, 'She's daft to re-fuse the Laird o' Cock-pen!'

*pronounced 'dumfoon'er'd'

37. Up in the morning early

Words by ROBERT BURNS (1759-1796)

COLD AND RAW
arr. G.C.M.

1. Cauld blaws the wind frae east to west; The drift is driving sairly. Sae loud and shrill I hear the blast, I'm sure it's winter fairly.
2. The birds sit chitt-'ring in the thorn, A' day they fare but sparely; And lang's the nicht frae e'en to morn, I'm sure it's winter fairly.

© The Hardie Press 1994   Photocopying this copyright material is ILLEGAL.

The origin of the air is uncertain, but in 1692 Purcell used it as a ground bass and it also appears in *The Beggar's Opera*.

38. The spinning wheel

Ancient text of unknown origin

Melody by Mrs D.V. Thomson
arr. G.McP.

Allegretto ($\dotted\quarter = c.58$)

simile

1. As I sat at my spin-ning wheel, A bon-nie lad-die pass'd me by; As I sat at my spin-ning wheel, A
(2.) snow-white hands he did ex-tol, And praised my fin-gers neat and small; My snow-white hands he did ex-tol, And
(3.) said, 'Lay by your rock, your reel, Your win'-ings and your spin-ning wheel,' He said, 'Lay by your rock, your reel, Your

bonnie laddie pass'd me by. I turn'd me round and
praised my fingers neat and small. He said there was nae
win'ings and your spinning wheel.' He bade me lay them

view'd him weel, For oh he had a glancing e'e, My
lady fair, That e'en wi' me he could compare, His
a' aside, And come and be his bonnie bride; An'

poco rit.

a tempo

panting heart began to feel, But aye I turn'd my
words into my heart did steal, But aye I turn'd my
oh I lik'd his looks sae weel, I laid aside my

sim.

spin - - - - ning wheel, My pant-ing heart be-gan to feel, But
spin - - - - ning wheel, His words in-to my heart did steal, But
spin - - - - ning wheel, An' oh I lik'd his looks sae weel, I

Verses 1 & 2

aye I turn'd my spin-ning wheel. 2. My
aye I turn'd my spin-ning wheel. 3. He

Verse 3

laid a-side my

poco rit.   a tempo

spin-ning wheel.

rit.

39. What's a' the steer, kimmer?

Words anon.

Melody of Strathspey origin
arr. G.McP.

Poco agitato ($\quarternote = c.94$)

1. What's a' the steer, kimmer, What's a' the steer? Char-lie he is land-ed And haith! he'll soon be here; The win' was at his back, Carle, The win' was at his back, I

(2.) richt glad to hear't, kimmer, I'm richt glad to hear't, I hae a guid braid claymore An' for his sake I'll wear't. Sin' Char-lie he is land-ed, We hae nae mair to fear, Sin'

can-na sin' he's come, Carle, We were - na worth a plack. 2. I'm
Char-lie he is come, kim- mer, 'Tis a jub'- lee year.

The air was published with anonymous words in *The Scottish Minstrel* of 1821. Later, however, the words were attributed to Robert Allan of Kilbarchan and may relate to the escape of Lord Maxwell of Nithsdale from the Tower of London in 1715 'dressed in a woman's cloak and hood, which were for some time after called Nithsdales'.

40. Wilt thou be my dearie?

Words by ROBERT BURNS (1759-1796)

THE SOUTER'S DAUGHTER
arr. J.R.

Affettuoso ($\quarternote = c.52$)

1. Wilt thou be my dear - ie? When
2. Las - sie, say thou lo'es me; Or,

© The Hardie Press 1994   Photocopying this copyright material is ILLEGAL.

sor - row wrings thy gen - tle heart, O wilt thou let me cheer thee?
if thou will na be my ain, O say na thou'lt re - fuse me;

By the trea - sures of my soul, That's the love I bear thee! I
If it win - na, can - na be, Thou, for thine, may choose me; O

swear and vow that on - ly thou Shall e - ver be my dear - ie.
let me, las - sie, quick - ly dee, Still trust - ing that thou lo'es me.

On - ly thou, I swear and vow, Shall e - ver be my dear - ie.
Las - sie, let me quick - ly dee, Still trust - ing that thou lo'es me.

41. The wee wee German lairdie

Words by ALLAN CUNNINGHAM (1784-1842)

ANDRO AND HIS CUTTY GUN
arr. J.R.

Giocoso (♩ = c. 96)

1. Wha the de'il ha'e we got-ten for a king, But a wee wee Ger-man laird - ie, And when we gaed to bring him hame, He was del-ving in his kail yaird - ie. He was sheugh-in' kail and
2. And he's clap-pit down in our gude-man's chair, The wee wee Ger-man laird - ie, And he's brought fouth o' for-eign trash, And dibbled them in his yaird - ie, He's pu'd the rose o'

© The Hardie Press 1994

Photocopying this copyright material is ILLEGAL.

lay - in' leeks With - out the hose, and but the breeks, And
Eng - lish loons, And bro - ken the harp o' Ir - ish clowns, But

up his beg - gar duds he cleeks, This wee wee Ger - man laird - ie.
our Scots thistle will jag his thumbs, The wee wee Ger - man laird - ie.

Verses 1-3

Verse 4

laird - ie.

3. Come up amang our Highland hills
   Thou wee wee German lairdie,

   And see how the Stuarts' lang kail thrive,

   They dibbled in our yairdie:
   And if a stock thou daur to pu',
   Or hand the yokin' o' a plough,
   We'll break your sceptre owre your mou',
   Thou wee bit German lairdie!

4. Auld Scotland thou'rt owre cauld a hole
   For nursin' siccan vermin;
   But the very dogs o' England's court
   They bark and howl in German.

   They keep thy dibble in thy ain hand,
   Thy spade but and thy yairdie,
   For wha' the de'il now claims your land
   But a wee wee German lairdie!

42. We're a' noddin'

Words anon.
Taken from *The Book of Scottish Song*

NID NODDIN'
arr. S.M.R.

Allegretto a piacere (♩ = c.108)

leggiero

p leggiero

And we're a' nod-din', nid, nid, nod-din', And we're a' nod-din' at our house at hame.

Last time to 𝄌

1. Gude e'en to ye, kim-mer, And are ye a-lane? O
2. O sair ha'e I fought, Ear' and late did I toil, My
3. When he knocket at the door, I thocht I kent the rap, And

© The Hardie Press 1994   Photocopying this copyright material is ILLEGAL.

come and see how blythe are we, For Jamie he's cam' hame; And
bairn-ies for to feed and clead' My con-fort was their smile; When I
lit-tle Ka-tie cried a-loud, 'My dad-die he's cam' back!' A

(Verse 3 rall.)

O, but he's been lang a-wa', And O, my heart was sair, As I
thocht on Jamie far a-wa', An' o' his love sae fain, A
stoun gaed through my anx-ious breast, As thocht-full-y I sat, I

a tempo) **D. S.**

sob-bed out a lang fare-weel, May-be to meet nae mair.
bod-in' thrill cam' through my heart We'd may-be meet a-gain. *Noo we're*
raise— I gazed—fell in his arms, And burst-ed out and grat.

rall. *poco lento*

dim.

43. When the kye comes hame

Words by JAMES HOGG (1770-1835)

THE BLATHRIE O'T
arr. G.McP.

Moderato ($\quarternote = c.63$)

1. Come all ye jolly shepherds, That whistle thro' the glen, I'll tell ye o' a secret That courtiers dinna ken. What is the greatest bliss That the tongue o' man can name? 'Tis to
2. 'Tis not beneath the burgonet Nor yet beneath the crown, 'Tis not on couch o' velvet, Nor yet on bed o' down; 'Tis beneath the spreading birch, In the dell without a name, Wi' a
3. A-wa' wi' fame and fortune What comforts can they gi'e? And a' the arts that prey upon man's life and libertie! Gi'e me the highest joy That the heart o' man can frame, My

© The Hardie Press 1994

Photocopying this copyright material is ILLEGAL.

woo a bon-nie las-sie, When the kye comes hame.
bon-nie, bon-nie las-sie, When the kye comes hame. *When the kye comes hame,—When the*
bon-nie, bon-nie las-sie, When the kye comes hame.

kye comes hame, 'Tween the gloam-in' and the mirk, When the kye comes hame.

[Verse 3]
kye comes hame.

In *The Popular Songs and Melodies of Scotland* Farquhar Graham claims that these words are not by Hogg, but are an earlier version. Graham also points out that Hogg 'considerably altered' the air.

44. Willie's gane tae Melville Castle

Words anon.

Origin of melody unknown
arr. G.McP.

Marziale ($\quarter = c.100$)

1. O Willie's gane tae Melville Castle, Boots and spurs an' a'; Tae bid the leddies a' fare-weel, Before he gaed awa'. Willie's young and Willie's bonnie, Liked by ane an' a'; O! She
2. The first he met was Lady Kate, Who led him thro' the ha'; And wi' a sad and sorry heart She let the tears doun fa'. Beside the fire stood Lady Grace, Said ne'er a word ava';

© The Hardie Press 1994

Photocopying this copyright material is ILLEGAL.

what will a' the las-ses do, When Wil-lie gaes a-wa'?
thought that she was sure o' him, Be-fore he gaed a-wa'.

After last verse

3. The next he saw was Lady Bell,
   'Gude troth ye need na craw,
   Maybe the lad will fancy me,
   And disappoint ye a'.'
   Then doun the stair stepp'd Lady Jean;
   The flow'r amang them a'.
   'Oh! lasses trust in Providence,
   And ye'll get husbands a'!'

4. As on his steed he gallop'd off,
   They a' cam' to the door,
   He gaily rais'd his feather'd plume;
   They set up sic a roar!
   Their sighs, their cries brought Willie back;
   He kiss'd them ane an' a';
   'Oh! lasses bide till I come hame,
   And then I'll take ye a'.'

45. Will ye no' come back again?

Words by LADY NAIRNE (1766-1845)

Traditional melody
arr. J.R.

Andante (♩ = c.96)

1. Bon - nie Char - lie's noo a - wa'; Safe - ly owre the friend - ly main; Mo - ny a heart will break in twa, Should he ne'er come
2. Ye trust - ed in your Hie - lan' men, They trust - ed you, dear Char - lie! They kent your hid - ing in the glen, Death or ex - ile
3. Sweet's the lave - rock's note and lang Lift - ing wild - ly up the glen; But aye to me he sings ae sang, Will ye no' come

© The Hardie Press 1994

Photocopying this copyright material is ILLEGAL.

back   a - gain.
brav - ing.   *Will ye no' come back a - gain?*
back   a - gain?

Will ye no' come back a - gain? Bet-ter lo'ed ye can-na be, Will ye no' come back a - gain?

Glossary

adj. adjective; *n.* noun;
adv. adverb; *prep.* preposition;
conj. conjunction; *pron.* pronoun;
int. interjection; *v.* verb.

a' *adj.* all
ado *v.* to do
aboot *prep.* about
abune *adv./prep.* above
ae (ane) *n./adj.* one, only
aff *adv.* off
aft(en) *adv.* often
ain *adj.* own
alane *adj.* alone
ance *adv.* a short while
auld *adj.* old
ava *adv.* at all
awa *adv.* away

bairn *n.* child
baith *adj.* both
barefit *adj.* barefooted
barley-bree *n.* whisky
bawk *n.* strip of unploughed land
behin' *adv.* behind
ben *adv.* in, inside
bide *v.* live, stay
bigg *v.* build
binge *v.* curtsy
blaw *v.* blow
blink *n.* wink
boden *adj.* prepared
bonnie(y) *adj.* handsome
bothy *n.* cottage for farm servants
boun *v.* bound
brachen *n.* bracken, fern
brae *n.* bank
braid *adj.* broad
braw *adj.* handsome
breeks *n.* trousers
bricht *adj.* bright
briest-knot *n.* a bow or ribbon worn on the chest
broun *adj.* brown
burgonet *n.* linen cap or coif

ca' *v.* call
cam' *v.* came
canna *v.* cannot

cannie *adj.* careful
carl(e) *n.* lad, fellow
cauld *adj.* cold
chittering *v.* shivering
Christendie *n.* Christendom
claise *n.* clothes
clappit *v.* sat down
clead *v.* clothe
cleeks *v.* grabs, catches up
cloot *n.* garment
coft *v.* bought
cot-town *n.* humble farm house
couthie(y) *adj.* kind
craw *v.* crow
crawberry *n.* crowberry
creepie *n.* low footstool
croose *adj.* bold

daff *v.* make sport
daur *v.* dare
daurna *v.* dare not
daw *v.* dawn
dawt *v.* caress
deal *n.* board
deave *v.* deafen
dee *v.* die
de'il *n.* devil
dibble *v.* plant
din *n.* loud noise
dine *n.* dinner time
dinna *v.* do not
dirl'd *v.* 'struck up'
dochter *n.* daughter
doon (doun) *prep.* down
dow nocht *v./n.* do nothing
drablit *adj.* made wet and dirty
drap *n.* drop
duds *n.* shabby clothes
dumfounder'd *v.* dumfounded

e'e (e'en) *n.* eye or eyes
e'en *n.* evening
eneuch *n./adj.* enough

fa' *v.* fall
fain *adj.* fond
faither *n.* father
fand *v.* find
fareweel *n.* farewell
farl *n.* quarter section of an oatcake
fashous *adj.* difficult
faulds *n.* sheep folds
fee *v.* hire
fere (fiere) *n.* friend
fit *n.* foot
flee *v.* fly
floo'r *n.* flower
forbye *prep.* besides, also
forgat *v.* forgot
forgie *v.* forgive
fou *adj.* drunk
fouth *n.* plenty
frae *prep.* from

gae (gang) *v.* go
gar *v.* make
gate *n.* way
gaudy *adj.* mischievous
gear *n.* dress, possessions
gie, gi'en *v.* give, given
gin *conj.* if
gird *n.* blow
glent *v.* peep out
gloamin' *n.* twilight
gloom *v.* despise
glower *v.* scowl, stare
goun *n.* gown
gowan *n.* daisy
gowd *n.* gold
grat *v.* cried
gratefu' *adv.* gratefully
gravat *n.* cravat
greet *v.* cry
gude (guid) *n./adj.* God, good
gudeman *n.* husband or landlord

ha' *n.* hall, house
haddin *n.* stock or furniture
ha'e *v.* have
hame *n.* home
haith *int.* faith!
haplie *adv.* wrapped up
harrie *adj.* stubborn
haud *v.* hold
heid *n.* head

herd *v.* tend cattle
hielan' *adj.* highland
hielands *n.* highlands
hoo *adv.* how
hoor *n.* hour
hoose *n.* house
huist *n.* heap

ilk(a) *adj.* like, each
ilka *adj.* lordly, very liberal
ither *adj.* other

jad, jaud *n.* jade
jo *n.* sweetheart

kail *n.* type of cabbage
kail-yaird *n.* kitchen garden
ken *v.* know
kenn'd (kent) *v.* knew
kimmer *n.* gossip
kirtle *n.* dress
knocket *v.* knocked
knowes *n.* hillocks
kye *n.* cattle

laigh *adj.* low
lane *adv.* alone
lang *adj.* long
laveroch *n.* lark
law *adv.* low
lea *v.* leave
leal *adj.* faithful
lee'in *v.* lying
lee-lang *adj.* livelong
licht *v.* alight
lift *n.* sky
lo'e *v.* love
lood *adj.* loud
loon *n.* fellow, rascal
loot *v.* let, allowed
lour *v.* lurk
lowlan's *n.* lowlands

mak' *v.* make
mailen *n.* small holding
mair *adj.* more
mankie *n.* calamanco
maun *v.* must
maut *n.* malt
mawn *n.* basket
meikle (mickle) *adj.* large, much

Mess John *n.* minister
micht *v.* might
min' *v.* to mind
minnie *n.* mother
mirk *n.* night
mither *n.* mother
mony *adj.* many
mou' *n.* mouth
muckle *adv.* much
murky *adj.* dark
mutch *n.* woman's cap

nae *adj./adv.* no, none, not
naething *n.* nothing
nane *adj.* none
neebor *n.* neighbour
neist *adj./adv.* next
nicht *n.* night
no' *adv.* not
nocht *n.* nought
noo *adv.* now

o' *int.* oh!
oor *n.* hour
oor *pron.* our
ought *adj.* eight
owre (o'er) *adv.* too, over
owsen *n.* oxen

paidelt *v.* paddled
pint-stoup *n.* drinking vessel
plack *n.* smallest coin
plaidie *n.* plaid
pouther'd *v.* powdered
prie *v.* taste
proffer *n.* offer of marriage
prood *adj.* proud
pu'd *v.* pulled
puir *adj.* poor

richt *adv.* right
rin *v.* run
rock *n.* distaff
rockley *n.* short cloak
rowed (row'd) *v.* rolled, wrapped
rowin' *adv.* rolls

sae *adv.* so
sair *adj.* sore
sairly *adv.* severely
sang *n.* song

sauf *v.* save
saut *n./adj.* salt
saxpence *n.* sixpence
scroggie *adj.* stunted
service *n.* toast
shauchled(i't) *adj.* distorted
shaw *n.* grove
sheughin *v.* digging
shield *n.* shepherd's hut
shoon (sheen) *n.* shoes
shouther *n.* shoulder
sic *adj.* such
siccan *adj.* such-like
siller *n.* silver (money)
simmer *n.* summer
sin' *adv.* since
sma' *adj.* small
sodgerin' *v.* soldiering
spak *v.* spoke
speer *v.* ask
spring *n.* lively tune
steek *v.* close, shut
steer *n.* commotion
sten *v.* spring up
stoun *n.* throb of pain
strake *v.* stroke
sune *adv.* soon
syne *adv.* then, ago

tae *prep.* to
tak (ta'en) *v.* take, taken
tassie *n.* small glass
teddling *v.* spreading out
tent *v.* herd animals
thegither *adv.* together
thocht *n./v.* thought
thraws *n.* pains
ticht *adj.* neat
till't *prep.* to it
timmer *n.* trees
tine *v.* lose
tither *adj.* other
tocher *n.* dowry
tocherband *n.* deed signed in connection with a dowry
toon *n.* town
troth *n.* truth
trow *v.* feel sure
twa *n.* two
'twad *pron./v.* it would

unco *adv.* very

wad *v.* would
wae's me *int.* woe is me
wan *v.* won
warld *n.* world
wat *v.* wager
waur *adj.* worse
wee *adj.* small, little
weel *adj.* well
weel stockit mailin *n.* well-stocked farm
wha(m) *pron.* who(m)
wi' *prep.* with
wil'd *v.* lured

win *v.* reside
win' *n.* wind
win awa *v.* get away
winna *v.* will not
woo *v.* court
wow *int.* exclamation of surprise

yestreen *n.* last evening
yett *n.* gate
yird *n.* earth
yon *adj.* those
yowes *n.* ewes

Index of Titles and First Lines

(First lines are in italic)

	SONG NO.
A rosebud by my early walk	1
And ye shall walk in silk attire	2
As I sat at my spinning wheel	38
Auld lang syne	3
Be gude to me	4
Blythe ha'e I been on yon hill	5
Blythe was the time	6
Bonnie Charlie's noo awa'	45
Braw, braw lads	10
Cauld blaws the wind frae east to west	37
Come all ye jolly shepherds	43
Come owre the stream, Charlie	8
Gae bring tae me a pint o' wine	9
Gala Water	10
Glenlogie	7
Hey, the bonnie briest-knots!	11
How pleasant the banks of the clear winding Devon	30
I lo'e nae a laddie but ane	12
I'll bid my heart be still	13
I'm owre young to marry yet	17
Jock o' Hazeldean	14
Last May a braw wooer	15
Leezie Lindsay	18
Logie o' Buchan	20
Muirland Willie	21
My heart's in the Highlands	23
My only jo and dearie, o	25
O Bothwell bank	19
O hearken and I will tell you hoo	21
O Willie brew'd a peck o' maut	26
Oh, Nancy's hair is yellow like gowd	24

	SONG NO.
On Ettrick's banks	27
Scots wha hae	28
Sheep and cattle I ha'e nane, O	35
Should auld acquaintance be forgot	3
The banks of the Devon	30
The bonnie Earl o' Moray	22
The carls o' Dysart	31
The gallant weaver	32
The gloomy night is gath'ring fast	33
The Laird o' Cockpen	36
The lass of Patie's mill	34
The Rowan Tree	16
The spinning wheel	38
The tocherless lass	35
The wee wee German lairdie	41
Thou has left me ever, Jamie	29
Three score o' nobles rade up the King's ha'	7
Thy cheek is o' the rose's hue	25
Up in the morning early	37
We're a' noddin'	42
Wha the de'il ha'e we gotten for a king	41
What's a' the steer, kimmer?	39
When the kye comes hame	43
Where Cartrins row in tae the sea	32
Why weep ye by the tide Ladye?	14
Will ye gang to the Hielands, Leezie Lindsay?	18
Will ye no' come back again?	45
Willie's gane tae Melville Castle	44
Wilt thou be my dearie?	40
Ye hielan's an' ye lowlan's	22